MORE THAN CONQUERORS

MORE THAN
CONQUERORS

Missionary Stories from South America

by
HELEN TEMPLE

NAZARENE PUBLISHING HOUSE
Kansas City, Missouri

FIRST PRINTING, 1967

PRINTED IN THE
UNITED STATES OF AMERICA

Preface

The spoken witness, the Word of God, the personal example of living Christian love—these were the avenues through which the people of this book were won to Christ, and became "more than conquerors" through the power of the Holy Spirit.

They are representative of hundreds of other faithful Christians in South America who are winning men and women to Christ through their faithful and victorious witness to His saving power.

I am indebted to Mrs. Jerry Demetre, Mrs. Ira Taylor, Miss Margaret Primrose, Rev. Howard Conrad, Rev. Clyde Golliher, Mrs. Ardee Coolidge, Mr. Klein DeBow, and others for story and background material which has been used in these stories. They have taken time from their crowded schedules to provide the information which has made these stories possible. I am deeply grateful for their help.

—H. F. T.

Contents

1

ARGENTINA

Ye Shall Be My Witnesses

Gingerly, twelve-year-old Emilio balanced another shoe last on the precarious tower he was building at the end of his father's cobbler bench. He released his hold carefully, both hands ready to catch the tower if it started to topple.

"Emilio!"

Emilio jumped at his father's shout, and the pile of lasts clattered to the bench and off onto the floor. He stooped quickly to retrieve them.

"You good-for-nothing rascal! Get out of here!" his father roared, his moustache quivering with anger. "Never mind picking them up. Just get out! Quick! Out of the shop! Out of my sight!"

He started toward Emilio and Emilio ducked, but not quickly enough. His father's hand struck him sharply on the side of the head. He ran from the little shoe-repair shop, rubbing his ear and fighting to keep back the tears. When he had been little, he could cry, and his mother would comfort him; but at twelve, boys didn't cry. Even if he had cried, there was no mother now to give him any comfort.

"That boy will ruin me yet!" Don Alberto grumbled, stomping back to his place. "I don't know what to do with him. Back home in Italy I could send him to his grandfather's. He could run off his energy in the fruit orchard. But here in Buenos Aires there is nothing for a boy his age to do."

He picked up his ever-present wine bottle and poured himself a drink. "Luigi!" he shouted to the young apprentice working at the other end of the little shop. "Pick up the mess the boy has made, and put the things back where they belong."

Luigi dropped his work and began to pick up the fallen shoe lasts. He did not say anything, for he had learned that silence was the best answer when Don Alberto was angry, which seemed to be most of the time.

Don Alberto pounded furiously with his tack hammer for a moment. Then he shouted again. "You, Luigi! Bring me another piece of leather."

"Yes, sir," Luigi answered quickly. He took a sheet of leather from the counter and carried it to his employer. "This is the last piece, sir. Do you want me to go and get more at the tanners?"

"And get me cheated out of my skin?" Alberto roared. "What do you know about buying good leather? You haven't been here six months, and now you think you are good enough to pick my leather for me. Next week I suppose you'll want to take over the shop!"

"No, sir," Luigi said quietly. "But I know you have a lot of orders to fill, and I wanted to help. I have tried to learn all the points you have taught me about good leather. I'll do my best not to get cheated."

Don Alberto grunted and worked on silently for a moment. Finally he looked up. "Well—somebody has to get it," he said reluctantly. "And I have ten pairs of shoes to repair before night. Go ahead! But get only one piece—the smallest you can find. I don't want to waste any more money than I have to."

Before Don Alberto had finished the shoe he had started, Luigi was back with the leather. He waited anxiously as Don Alberto bent it between his fingers, and turned it over several times to examine it.

"Well—he didn't cheat you this time," Don Alberto said grudgingly.

"He tried to sell me another piece, but I thought this one was better," Luigi said.

Don Alberto fingered the leather again. He hated to admit it, but the boy had chosen a piece every bit as good as he could have picked himself.

"It's good leather," he admitted. "Maybe you'll make a shoe man someday after all. But don't get any big ideas. You have a lot more to learn yet! Now get on back to your work."

Don Alberto glanced up occasionally to watch Luigi as he swept the shop and put the tools and supplies in their places. Not once did Don Alberto catch his apprentice idling. That's a most unusual boy for a fifteen-year-old, he thought, puzzled. He behaves like a good lad from the Old Country. I wish my own was more like him.

As the hands of the clock crept toward twelve noon, Don Alberto put down his work. He went to the door and looked out.

"Emilio!" he shouted. "That good-for-nothing boy is under my feet when I'm working, and when I want him he can't be found," he fumed.

"He was sitting on the bench by the door when I came back from the tanner's," Luigi said quietly. "He can't be far away."

"Emilio!" Don Alberto shouted again.

"I'm right here, Father."

Don Alberto jerked his head around to where Emilio stood on the other side of the door. "Well, why didn't you say something, not just stand there like a dolt! Here." He handed him a coin. "Go to the pastry maker's and get three empanadas. And hurry!"

Emilio darted off. His father closed the shop door and drew down the blinds.

Luigi picked up his jacket and started to leave.

"There's no need for you to waste the whole noon hour traveling across town for your lunch," Don Alberto said gruffly. "Eat with Emilio and me. It won't be much, but it will save you that long trip."

Luigi looked at him, startled. Everyone went home for lunch in Buenos Aires, no matter how far away he lived. Sometimes, when people lived in the suburbs as he did, there was scarcely time to gulp a bowl of soup before starting back. But it was almost unheard of for an employer to invite his workers to eat with him.

"Thank you, sir," he stammered. "It's very kind of you."

"Nonsense! I'm protecting myself. I want to be sure you are back here in time to go to work when we open up again at two-thirty."

Luigi followed his employer upstairs to the three rooms above the shop that were home for Don Alberto and Emilio.

By the time Don Alberto had put plates and knives and forks on the table, Emilio was home with the hot empanadas.

It was the kind of meal a motherless household might be expected to have: a loaf of crusty Italian bread, a wedge of sharp cheese, the inevitable bottle of wine, and the hot, savory meat pies from the pastry shop.

"Help yourself to bread and cheese," Don Alberto said brusquely, as he put the pies on the three plates. "Here, let me pour you some wine." He reached for Luigi's glass.

"No, thank you, sir," Luigi said timidly.

"Oh, come now, you needn't be afraid to drink my wine," Don Alberto said jovially. "If you are old enough to work, you are old enough to enjoy a little good wine." He tipped the bottle to pour it into Luigi's glass.

"No, thank you, sir," Luigi said again. "I don't care for any."

Don Alberto was impressed. This young lad was not only a good worker—he was polite. Not many young chaps had learned to refuse food that was offered to them the polite two times before accepting.

"I insist," he said, being the good host. "You must have a glass of wine. It will give you strength."

"I'm sorry, sir, but I don't want any," Luigi said, moving his glass away.

Don Alberto stopped with the bottle in midair. "Twice is enough, young man," he reprimanded sharply. "You are insulting me now."

"I don't mean to, sir," Luigi said, trembling. "But I am telling the truth. I don't drink wine."

Don Alberto's face turned crimson with anger. For a moment Luigi thought he was going to strike him over the head with the wine bottle.

"You are a foolish and obstinate donkey!" Don Alberto shouted angrily. "If I say you are old enough to drink wine—you are old enough. Now give me that glass." He pulled the glass from Luigi's hand and filled it with wine. "Drink it!" he ordered.

"You don't understand, sir," Luigi said. "I don't drink wine because I'm a Christian."

Don Alberto dropped the bottle to the table with a thump. "Oh, you are, are you! And what do you think I am, an animal? Young man, I was baptized before you were born! I never heard of a man not drinking wine. Even the priest drinks wine. Do you think you are better than he is?"

"But I am an *evangelico*," Luigi answered. "We don't drink wine because we don't think it is good for people. We want to be at our best for God, and we don't think we can if our wits are dulled by liquor."

Don Alberto stared at him. Twice he opened his mouth to speak, but no sound came. He sat down heavily in his chair. "I never heard of such a thing," he said at last. "Whoever taught you to believe such tommyrot?"

"It is what all *evangelicos* believe," Luigi answered.

"Humph!" Don Alberto snorted. He poured the wine into his own glass and drank it. "I suppose you think I shouldn't drink it either," he said.

"I think you might not be bothered by things so much if you didn't drink," Luigi said bravely, fully expecting a clip on the ear for his boldness.

Don Alberto stopped with his fork halfway to his mouth. He looked at Luigi. Never in his life had he heard such ideas from a youngster like this one. He shook his head and resumed eating. At last he said, "Where did you say you go to church?"

"In Castelar," Luigi said. "To the evangelical church."

"Queer people!" Don Alberto muttered. "Very queer people. But you're a good worker; that's all I care."

He began to clear up the table. "Emilio, do the dishes. Luigi, you have time for a little siesta before we open the shop again. And you might as well plan to eat lunch with us every day."

"Thank you, sir," Luigi faltered, stunned by this unexpected kindness.

The following Monday, when Luigi finished eating, instead of taking a siesta, he pulled a paper from his pocket and began to read it.

"What do you have there, boy?" Don Alberto asked curiously.

"A paper from my Sunday school," Luigi answered.

"What kind of a paper?" Don Alberto asked. "Read it to me."

Luigi read him the Bible story in his paper.

Don Alberto made no comment when Luigi finished. Indeed he seemed unusually quiet through most of the afternoon.

Working at his own end of the cobbler's bench, Luigi hummed softly to himself the songs he had learned in Sunday school.

Toward the end of the afternoon Don Alberto looked up. "What is that tune you are humming?" he asked. "It sounds like one I used to sing in Italy when I was a young man."

Luigi sang the words.

"It's a very pretty tune," Don Alberto said. "Do you know any more?"

Luigi sang more of the choruses and hymns of his church. Once he thought he caught a glimpse of tears in Don Alberto's eyes, but he pretended not to see. He stopped singing and bent over his work.

"Don't you know any more songs?" Don Alberto asked after a moment. "Singing takes me back to the days in Italy when I was young. I used to sing for my girl when I courted her."

He stared at the wall for a moment, lost in his memories; then abruptly picked up his hammer and began to work furiously.

Every day after that he asked Luigi to sing as they worked.

"I think you would like to visit our church," Luigi said one day. "We sing these songs together. You could sing with us."

"Oh, no," Don Alberto answered quickly. "I would have no place in a church like yours. And besides, there's no song in my heart anymore, since Emilio's mother died—God rest her soul." He turned his back

15

lest Luigi should see him brush his hand across his eyes, and began to work very diligently on a shoe.

Every week Luigi invited Don Alberto to come to church with him on Sunday. And every week Don Alberto thought of a new reason why he could not go. It seemed hopeless to keep on asking.

But one week Don Alberto surprised Luigi. "If you will come in for us, Emilio and I will go to church with you Sunday," he said, just as Luigi was leaving.

Don Alberto and Emilio were just finishing their coffee-with-milk and toast when Luigi knocked at the door the next morning.

"You're here early, my friend," Don Alberto said, opening the door. "I thought your church did not begin until ten."

"It doesn't," Luigi admitted, "but I wanted to be sure I was here in time, so that we would not be late getting back."

Don Alberto became increasingly nervous as the bus traveled across the city. He fidgeted and twisted on the seat, and ran his finger around inside his collar that was suddenly too tight. When they stepped off in front of the church, he looked around quickly to see if anyone on the street recognized him. He didn't go to his own church very often, but he certainly did not want anyone reporting to the priest that they had seen him going to this one.

Inside the church he glanced about him surreptitiously, but saw no one that he knew. He relaxed a little, looking around at the plain, bare room. What an odd building for a church! There was nothing in it— no saints, no rich decorations, no stations of the Cross, no confessional—nothing at all but four bare walls and a plain platform on which two men sat, dressed in ordinary street clothes.

But when the people began to sing, the little building became alive. They sang joyously, triumphantly,

16

like—like what? He could not remember ever hearing music quite like this. Not even when he used to go to the operas in Italy with his wife. He felt as though he wanted to sing with them, and when they sang some of the songs Luigi had been singing in the shop, Don Alberto joined in.

Not for anything would he have admitted how deeply he was stirred by the words of the preacher as he explained God's Word. He thanked Luigi for inviting him, and rode home on the bus, silent and thoughtful.

Beside him Emilio chattered about the sights along the way. Don Alberto scarcely heard him.

He could not understand this strange church. Bare and unlovely compared to his own, it should have seemed cold, but there had been a strange, indefinable warmth that filled the whole room. It was more than the friendly people. There was something else. But he could not figure out what it was.

"How did you like my church?" Luigi inquired eagerly the next morning.

"It was very different," Don Alberto answered cautiously.

Then, seeing the disappointment in Luigi's face, he added, "The people certainly like to sing!"

"Yes, that's one of the best parts of our worship services—all the singing," Luigi said, beaming. "I'm glad you liked it. I hope you'll come with me again."

"Oh, I don't know about that," Don Alberto said quickly. "I have my own church, you know." Not for anything would he let Luigi know how much his heart was already drawn to the *evangelico* church. But as the week drew to a close, he waited anxiously for Luigi to invite him again.

For a while he was afraid Luigi would not do it. But at lunch on Friday, Luigi finally said, "Don Alberto, I would like to have you and Emilio come to my church

17

again Sunday. Would you? I'll be glad to come over and meet you."

"Oh, you wouldn't need to do that," Don Alberto remonstrated. "If we come, we can find our own way."

"I'll wait for you outside the church then," Luigi promised.

Luigi prayed many times between then and Sunday morning. He wanted to be sure that nothing kept Don Alberto and Emilio from coming to church.

On Sunday morning he stationed himself at the door right after breakfast and watched each bus that came in from Don Alberto's direction. He had almost given up hope of their coming when a bus stopped just as the service was beginning, and Don Alberto and Emilio stepped off.

Luigi hurried to welcome them.

"We caught a later bus, and it was very crowded," Don Alberto explained apologetically. "I think it stopped at every street."

Again the strange warmth of the *evangelico* service impressed him. As the preacher spoke of man's sinful ways and his need for salvation, he described Don Alberto's life with alarming accuracy. Don Alberto squirmed uncomfortably. Had Luigi been talking to the pastor? He looked at Luigi beside him. "What have you told him about me?" he demanded in a whisper.

"Nothing," Luigi said. "I haven't said a word except that I work for you."

Don Alberto settled back and listened again. He would have sworn that Luigi had talked to the pastor about him, but he had never caught the boy in a lie yet, and somehow he felt certain that Luigi wouldn't tell a lie.

It took only a few weeks of listening to the gospel messages for Don Alberto to discover that the discomfort he felt was the Holy Spirit talking to him. By this time he had also learned the remedy. At the close of a morning service he went to the altar in the little *evangelico* church and asked God to forgive his sins.

Emilio followed his father. He had wanted to give his heart to God from the beginning, but he had been afraid of what his father would do to him.

Things were much different in Don Alberto's home after that wonderful Sunday. The wine bottles disappeared from the table and the cobbler's bench. Don Alberto's fiery temper calmed down. For the first time since his mother had died, Emilio felt loved and wanted by his father.

They went to church every Sunday and every prayer meeting night, even though it meant closing the shoe-repair shop early in order to get there.

And then God added still another blessing to their new happiness. Don Alberto met a Christian widow in the *evangelico* church. They became friends, and in a few months they were married and Emilio once again had a complete family. It was good to come home to a mother who loved him, who cooked good meals and the special pastries and treats that only mothers seem to know how to make.

Two baby sisters were born in the years that followed. Don Alberto's happy Christian home was a shining example for Christ in their community as well as in the church.

As the children grew up, they gave their lives to God for His service. Emilio and his younger sister went to Bible school—Emilio to become a Nazarene pastor, and his sister to later find her place of service in a Nazarene parsonage as a preacher's wife. The older sister stayed at home, but became the district teen leader in the church.

And Luigi, the young apprentice whose courage in refusing to drink Don Alberto's wine had brought all this about, also found his place in God's service as a Nazarene pastor in another Argentine city.

2

BOLIVIA

Servant of God

Carlos shivered a little as he helped his father fill the sacks of *tunta* and chuno. He wasn't sure whether he was excited, or scared, or just cold. It could have been all three.

"Who will help Mother trample the potatoes to make chuno next year?" he asked. He had always hated the job, for it was hard work, spreading the potatoes out at night to freeze, and then walking over them, barefoot, after they thawed—round and round and round to squeeze out all the juice. Doing this day after day until the potatoes were dry and hard, and your feet were chapped and raw from the frost! He had thought he would be glad to escape from the task, but now it seemed terribly important that his mother should not be left without anyone to help her.

"Your sisters are big enough to help," his father said. "They are already helping with the spinning and weaving."

His mother came to the door of the small adobe house. "Remember, you must obey Uncle Mario and Aunt Rosa as though they were your own parents," she admonished, tugging his new knitted cap down over his ears. "And study very hard in school. We aren't sending you to La Paz just to have a good time."

"I will," Carlos promised readily. "I'm going to study very hard, and learn very much. And then I shall become very rich and buy you a big house in the city, with windows and a stove in every room."

His mother laughed at his boyish nonsense. "Just study hard and come home to teach school here in Tiquina and help your father," she said. "That will satisfy us."

Carlos looked around the dark, windowless home. Suddenly its thick mud walls and heavy thatched roof were warm and familiar and dear to him. Even his mother's small cooking fire, that never warmed the house enough to be comfortable, seemed cheerful and inviting. He didn't want to leave. Not for school, or to be rich and have a big house, or anything.

His mother gave him a gentle shove. "Your father is waiting," she said. "Don't delay. It's a long journey to La Paz. I'll knit you a new sweater when we shear the sheep. Your father can bring it to La Paz when he comes the next time."

Carlos brushed away the sudden tears of homesickness that filled his eyes, and stumbled outside.

The cold wind that seemed always to be blowing down from Mount Illimani made him pull his heavy wool poncho closer around him.

Below their house, at the foot of the mountain, the deep blue waters of Lake Titicaca glowed with the rosy colors of the sunrise. Fishermen were already on the shore, getting ready to launch their reed fishing boats. For a moment Carlos wished with all his heart that his father had never thought of sending him to school. This was home. He loved every bit of it—the beautiful lake, the towering mountains, the clusters of little adobe houses on the mountainside around the lake. Who could ever want to leave this place for any reason?

His father helped Carlos shoulder two of the sacks, then took the rest on his own shoulders and set off down the path. Carlos followed, looking about him with the acutely sensitive vision of a young boy who is leaving a beloved and familiar place for the unknown.

When they reached the lake shore, Carlos' father stopped and slid his burden to the ground. "You stay here with the sacks," he said to Carlos. "I'll see if I can get passage to the other side."

He walked to the docks and began to dicker with the boatmen.

Carlos slid his own sacks to the ground and looked about him. A cluster of fishermen were busy stowing their nets in their boats. At one side the big ferry lay beside the dock, ready for the trucks that would soon be coming on their way from Copacabana to La Paz, and would need to be ferried to the other shore. A patch on its huge flapping sail bore some English words, and the initials "U.S.A."

Carlos' father came back and began to hoist his sacks to his shoulders. "I have a boat," he said. "Quickly! Help me put our sacks aboard."

They climbed into the boat with two other early morning passengers, and the boatman pushed his little sailboat out to where the sails would catch the freshening breeze. Carlos shivered with excitement. He had been in the small reed fishing boats once or twice, but he had never sailed all the way across the straits before. The little boat bobbed over the choppy waves like a gull about to take wing. From out in the lake the town of Tiquina looked like a toy village curled around the deep bay from the San Pedro side to the San Pablo shore.

On the other side, Carlos and his father unloaded their sacks and carried them to the large dock where the big ferry would tie up. They squatted comfortably in the shelter of a building out of the wind, and visited with other travelers as they waited for a truck to come across on its way to La Paz.

There was no question whether one would come. Tiquina was on the only road to Copacabana and the famous shrine of the Virgin. Trucks came through Tiquina several times a day, carrying pilgrims to and from the shrine. Before the morning was half over, they saw the huge sail of the ferry fill with the wind, as it moved out into the strait with its load. Slowly it lumbered its way across the waves to the San Pablo side. Groaning and creaking, it eased up to the dock and the deck hands tossed out the heavy ropes and twisted them around the posts to hold it fast in its berth. The truck on board rolled slowly onto the dock. Carlos and his father piled their sacks of chuno and *tunta* into the truck bed and climbed aboard. Other travelers pushed their baskets and sacks on, too. There was no place to sit except on top of the cargo. Carlos balanced himself on the sacks of chuno. He could feel the hard, dry chips beneath him.

The truck driver started his motor with a roar that drowned out their voices, and they rolled out onto the road to La Paz. The road twisted and curved like an angry snake, as it followed the lake shore. The truck driver leaned on his horn and swept around the hairpin corners without slackening his speed.

Carlos clung to the sacks of chuno and tried not to look afraid. Trucks and cars coming from La Paz pulled over just barely enough to let them by, but neither slowed down for the other. At Huarina the truck pulled off the road and stopped. This was the checkpoint for all traffic. Cars and trucks were lined up waiting to show their permanent permits. The passengers slid down off the truck and crowded around the women who were selling food at little tables beside the road. Carlos'

23

father bought two crisp, fried trout and a bowl of hot soup for each of them. Then they climbed back up on their sacks of chuno for the rest of the trip to La Paz.

They left the winding road by the lake and took the road that ran straight across the wide, level stretches of the altiplano to La Paz. Carlos looked about him at the barren sweep of land reaching to the horizon. They passed a flock of sheep tended by a boy about his own age. It made him homesick for his own flock.

At midafternoon they reached the rim of the canyon wall above the city of La Paz. The truck driver stopped and some of his passengers got off, unloading their bags and baskets.

"We will get off here, too," Carlos' father said. "We could ride a little farther, but I want you to have your first glimpse of La Paz from here."

They walked over to the canyon rim. Below they could see the Aymara homes along the upper level, merging with stores and markets lower down, and below them the larger houses of the wealthy people of the city. Beyond the houses a river flowed lazily through the broad, deep valley at the bottom of the canyon. Green fields stretched away from it on either side. There were trees in the valley, and bright splashes of color around the homes of the wealthy that Carlos' father said were flowers.

Carlos gazed in silent amazement. He had never seen anything so beautiful in his life, not even on the shores of Lake Titicaca.

They followed the road over the canyon rim and started down. Just a few yards down the trail, they turned off into a side lane that led through the Aymara section of La Paz. His father stopped at one of the homes. "This is your uncle's house," he said. "You will live here and work for him as you go to school."

The gate swung suddenly open. "Welcome! Welcome!" Uncle Mario cried, embracing Carlos' father. He

24

put his hands on Carlos' shoulders. "And this is the boy who is going to live with us and go to school. He's a fine boy. Come inside." He led the way through the gate.

They stacked their sacks of chuno and *tunta* in the little shed where Uncle Mario kept his burro. "I'll sell these in the market tomorrow," Father said. "Then I can give you the money for Carlos schooling. There is a sack of chuno for you, too. It will help a little with his food, perhaps."

Carlos looked around him in wonder. Uncle Mario's house was much larger than their own little adobe home by the lake. There were rooms on all sides of the small courtyard in which they stood.

Aunt Rosa came to the door of one of the rooms. "Come right in," she invited. "I have some hot tea ready for you." Carlos followed his father and Uncle Mario into the kitchen. Aunt Rosa handed him a cup of steaming tea and a big piece of fresh bread. He sat down on the floor and ate hungrily. Somehow, staying with Aunt Rosa and Uncle Mario did not seem quite so dismal as he had first thought it would be.

While the men ate and sipped their tea and talked, Aunt Rosa worked at the stove. Carlos watched her with interest. The fragrance coming from the big pot over the fire made his mouth water.

"What are you cooking, Aunt Rosa?" he asked, finally, going to stand beside her.

"This is *pski* [pss-key]," she said. "Doesn't your mother make *pski*?"

"I don't know," Carlos said. "If she does, it never smells as good as this."

Aunt Rosa laughed. "You're hungry, Son," she said. "Hunger makes any food smell good. You wait. When you eat dinner, you will remember that your mother makes this too."

Carlos watched her as she cut up meat and onions

25

and potatoes and dropped them into the bubbling pot. The crushed quinua seeds in the water swirled up around the vegetables and meat. Mmmmm! He wondered how he could ever wait until time for dinner! He went back and sat down beside the men.

Hours later, it seemed to Carlos, Aunt Rosa brought them bowls of the steaming *pski*, now dry and thick, with hot, spicy sauce poured over it.

Carlos took a big spoonful. He looked up and smiled at Aunt Rosa. "I remember it now," he said. "But Mother puts sour-milk clabber on it."

"I do too sometimes," Aunt Rosa said. "But this chili sauce is best when you've been out in the cold wind all day."

The hot food and the warm, cozy kitchen made Carlos sleepy. He struggled to keep his eyes open, but in spite of himself his head nodded.

He awoke with a start when Aunt Rosa shook him gently. "You've had a long, weary day, Carlos," she said. "Come, I'll show you where you are to sleep. You will want to be rested for your first day of school."

She led him across the courtyard to the sleeping room. On his bed were layers of bright-striped woolen blankets. "Slip under those and I think you'll be warm enough," she said. "It gets pretty chilly here in the night."

Carlos crawled under the warm homespun covers and in a moment he was sound asleep. He never heard his father and his uncle and aunt come to bed.

In the morning they had an early breakfast of black, sweet coffee and bread before Carlos' father went to the market. Carlos watched his father wistfully, as he gathered the sacks of chuno and *tunta* to take to market. He knew that when he came home from school his father would already be on his way back home to Tiquina. "Do you need me to help you, Father?" he asked hopefully.

"No, Son," his father replied. "You need to get started in school. I'll manage all right. You be a good boy, and help your Uncle Mario all you can. He is doing you a great favor to let you live here and go to school."

"I know," Carlos said. "I'll help. When will you come back again?"

"I may be back after the potato harvest, if we have chuno and wool to sell," Father said. "It is too far to come without a good reason."

He stood up with the load of sacks on his back, pulled his wool cap down over his ears, and went out the gate toward the market.

Carlos stood at the gate and watched his father until he disappeared from sight.

"Time to wash and get ready for school," Aunt Rosa called cheerfully.

Carlos turned slowly and went into the kitchen. He wanted to ask if Uncle Mario was going with him this first day, but he didn't dare. Aunt Rosa might think he was a baby. But he was a little scared about going to a city school all alone.

Before he had dried his face and hands, he heard a voice calling, "Dona Rosa, is Carlos ready yet?"

"Come in, Luis," Aunt Rosa said. "Carlos, this is Luis, from next door. He goes to the same school you will attend. He will stop for you every day."

Suddenly everything was all right. Luis introduced Carlos to his teacher, and helped him with his lessons. He made sure that the other boys included Carlos in their games at recess. In a few days Carlos felt as though he had always gone to school in La Paz.

After school he helped Uncle Mario in his garden plot on the rim of the canyon above the business section.

One day as Carlos was coming home from school without his friend Luis, he saw a crowd of people standing in the street. There was music coming from somewhere inside the group. Carlos pushed his way through the crowd until he was near the front. The people were listening to a small group who were playing trumpets and singing. After a while a man stood up and read from a Book. He told them that Jesus Christ loved the Aymara people of Bolivia, and that He would help them to live better lives, if they would let Him.

Carlos was mystified. He had never seen anyone like these people before. "Who are they?" he said to the man standing beside him.

"Shhh! They are *evangelicos,*" the man whispered. Carlos puzzled over the strange word. He had never heard of *evangelicos* before. A strange feeling came over him. He wished he were like these folks who were standing here singing about Jesus. Someday, he said to himself, when I grow up, I am going to be an *evangelico.* But he was much too shy to tell anyone about his resolve.

The year went by very swiftly for Carlos in La Paz. Soon school was over and it was time for him to go home. He was almost sorry to leave Uncle Mario and Aunt Rosa and all of his friends at school. But he had not seen his mother for twelve months, and his father had come to La Paz only once during the year. He would be glad to see them again.

He set out early one morning, after many good-byes for his friends and his aunt and uncle. From the top of the canyon rim he looked back down into the city. It had become his second home. He would miss it very much. Then he turned and climbed aboard the truck that was going to Copacabana.

They churned their way across the bleak altiplano, leaving a trail of billowing dust behind them. At Huarina, Carlos bought some buns from the women at their tables, while the driver stopped at the checkpoint. The road began to wind its way along the lake shore from Huarina, twisting and turning with many blind curves. Carlos remembered his fright when he had come this way the year before. He felt much older and wiser now.

He noticed the little clusters of windowless adobe houses along the road. They seemed much smaller than before. Would his own home look as small as these, he wondered.

The heavy truck lumbered around the last hairpin curve, its horn blaring, and Carlos saw Lake Titicaca spread out before him, blue and sparkling in the clear mountain air. He had forgotten how beautiful it was. Now he felt that he was home—really home! La Paz was wonderful, but it was not like this. He leaned forward searching for familiar landmarks. He saw the reed fishing boats on the water, the shops and houses along the edge of the lake. He could hear the shouts of little children playing in the streets.

The truck pulled up at the ferry dock and stopped. Carlos climbed down stiffly, and went to find someone who would take him across the straits for the little bit of money he had left. He found a sailboat that was just ready to leave. The owner had a load of passengers, but he agreed to take Carlos too. As the boat drew near to the San Pedro side, Carlos scanned the hillside, searching for the first glimpse of his own home. He sprang ashore, paid the boatman, and hurried up the trail to his father's house.

When he walked up to the door, his younger brothers and sisters looked up, startled. Then they realized who it was and ran shrieking to their mother with the news. She came hurrying to the door.

She looked older and grayer, Carlos noticed, and there was a stoop to her shoulders that he hadn't remembered. Perhaps she was tired from doing the work that he would have done if he had been home. Well, he was home now. He could take up the share of work that was rightfully his, again. He greeted his mother warmly.

"Where is Father?" he asked.

"Working in the fields with Manuel and Mario," she said, stepping back to look at her young son fondly. "He will be glad to see you home. The other boys are not really big enough to do a man's work yet."

Carlos pitched into the work with his father the next day. In a week it almost seemed as though he had never been away at all.

When the crops were all stored away in baskets and big clay jars for winter, Carlos had a little time to himself. He walked down to the village of Tiquina to see what changes had come while he had been away. There were a few new buildings. Some of his friends with whom he had been in school, he learned, were working with the fishing crews now. He wandered about the streets searching for someone he knew. Pushing open the gate to the home where one of his schoolmates had lived, he stepped into the patio before he discovered that there was a group of strangers there, and they were praying.

He stopped bewildered, wondering whether to run away or to wait and ask where his friend was.

"Young fellow, what are you looking for?" someone asked.

Carlos stammered the name of his friend who had formerly lived there.

"They have moved," another man said kindly. "They live over on the San Pablo side now."

"Thank you, Sir," Carlos said, backing out of the patio.

"Wait," the man called, holding out his hand. "We would like to invite you to our special meetings in the tent this afternoon."

"What kind of meetings?" Carlos asked curiously.

"Gospel meetings," the man replied. "We are *evangelicos*. We are just beginning special meetings here. We hope to have a church building before long."

Evangelicos! Carlos' mind flashed back to the group he had seen on the street in La Paz. That was what had seemed so familiar about these people in the patio. They were the same kind.

"Thank you," he said more warmly. "Perhaps I will come."

He hurried away in search of his friend. But in the afternoon he strolled over to the big brown tent where the gospel meetings were being held. There was a good crowd inside already. Many of the village people were there. Carlos went in hesitantly and sat down. The gospel message gripped his heart. Now he began to understand what the people on the street in La Paz had been talking about last year. When the preacher invited the people to come and pray for forgiveness for their sins, they streamed to the front from all over the tent. Trembling, Carlos went and knelt at the far end of the altar. The pastor and the few Christians who were there were kept busy praying with the many adults who were seeking God. No one noticed the young teen-ager kneeling at one side.

But God spoke to Carlos' heart that day. He did not fully understand what he needed, nor how to secure it. But he made up his mind that day that he was going to cast his lot with the *evangelicos.*

He went to every service the church held. Neither rain, nor snow, nor bitter cold could keep him away.

When his family discovered where he was going, they were very unhappy.

"Think of your older brother!" his mother admonished him. "He's the village witch doctor! What will people think when you go against him like this?"

"Think about us!" the other children cried. "Brother says that if you keep going to that group terrible things will happen to all of us."

"I gave you the privilege of going to school in La Paz so that you could better yourself," his father scolded. "Now you are throwing it all away to join that *evangelico* crowd. You will never get a decent job if you are known as one of them. You should be ashamed to repay your family like this, after we all sacrificed to give you a chance to learn."

But Carlos kept on going to church.

The pastor soon became aware of this young boy who came to every service, even the early morning prayer meetings that met at three-thirty.

As Carlos grew older, the pastor encouraged him to go to the Nazarene Bible College on the edge of La Paz. "It will help you spiritually," he said, "and I believe that there you will find God's plan for your life."

Carlos was not sure what to do. He wanted to go to Bible school. To live among Christians and learn more about the Bible would be a wonderful experience. But what about his family? Would they be won to Christ if he stayed home?

At last he decided to take his pastor's advice and go to the Bible school.

Once again he took the long truck ride into La Paz. He felt almost as shy and timid as he had when he first went to La Paz to go to elementary school. Bible school was a very different experience from anything he had known before.

Carlos did not find it easy to mix with the other young men in the school. He was quiet and kept to himself a good deal, spending much of his time studying. And it was there in Bible school, listening, and learning from his professors, that he at last understood the real meaning of salvation. Alone in his dormitory room, he knelt and prayed until he had the full assurance of forgiveness for all his sins.

Carlos was a very conscientious young man. If his temper flared in disagreement with a classmate or a teacher, he soon returned to beg forgiveness. If he felt

32

the Holy Spirit checking him on some hasty action, he quickly went back to straighten it out.

Though Carlos was not a brilliant student, he studied hard, and tried to prepare himself in every way he could for God's service. There was only one place where he gave up. He tried to take piano lessons and struggled with them for weeks, but could not seem to grasp the skill he needed. At last, after one discouraging session, he turned to his missionary-teacher and said, "*Señorita*, it appears that I'm studying piano in vain."

She had to agree, and to their mutual relief the lessons were dropped. But in all his other classes Carlos worked hard to master the subjects.

His ability for leadership began to show itself, not in flashy ways, but in spiritual insights that grasped the key to situations and helped him find the solutions.

His fellow students recognized this quality one evening in the study hall, and felt a new respect for their quiet friend. They had been unusually restless and talkative that evening, and the missionary in charge had not been able to quiet them down. As the time for devotions came, she could not capture the students' attention. She was about to close the period when Carlos stood to his feet. In his concern, he lapsed into the familiar Aymara language, and she could not follow what he was saying, but he captured the attention of the students. The shuffling and whispering ceased as every eye turned toward him. When he finished he said in Spanish, "Brothers, we're going to pray."

And pray they did! There was no indifference now. They fell on their knees and cried out to God with a concern that brought the Holy Spirit into their midst in blessing.

Carlos seemed quite unconscious of his influence upon his classmates. He continued to go his quiet way in their midst.

During one of the school revivals Carlos awakened

to his need for heart holiness and was sanctified wholly. He also found God's plan for his life—to preach the gospel.

In his last year at Bible school the missionaries sent him to pastor a small church not far from the school. Carlos loved this little flock like a true spiritual shepherd.

The school year was about half over when disaster struck, and threatened to make havoc of their promising corps of future pastors. A student came running to the school nurse one day in great excitement. "Juan is bleeding," he cried. "Come quickly!"

The nurse hurried to the dormitory. She had already guessed the dreaded truth, and her quick examination confirmed her fears. Tuberculosis! And in a very active stage!

Tuberculosis in a crowded dormitory, with students who were peculiarly susceptible to this disease sharing a common dining hall! She shuddered to think what might happen.

Every student and every missionary at the school had to go to the clinic for tests and X rays. Anxious days followed as they waited for the reports. It was hard to study or teach with the unknown answer so heavily on the mind of everyone. The students were fearful. They had seen many of their relatives die from this dreaded disease. As far as they knew, there was no hope for an Aymara when he became ill with it.

At last the school director was notified that he could come to the clinic for the reports. When he returned to the campus, one of the teachers asked eagerly, "How did they come out?"

"It's pretty bad!" he admitted. "Five more of our students have active cases of tuberculosis." He buried his face in his hands and wept.

It was a tragedy almost beyond comprehension. Five of their best students ill with tuberculosis! If the

34

disease was not arrested soon, they could well lose some, if not all, of these boys.

"What did the doctor say we should do?" the teacher asked fearfully. "Can we send the sick ones to the hospital?"

"There's no room at the hospital." The director groaned. "But the doctor did urge that we not send these boys home. They would surely die if we did. We know that. They could never get the care and medicine they need back there. The doctor said if we would isolate them and give them the medicine they need with plenty of rest and good food, he thought we could pull them out of it."

"Can we do that?" the teacher asked, startled. "How will we ever keep them isolated? You know the other boys will never believe these fellows are sick if they aren't confined to bed. And we'll have to boil all their dishes for months."

"I know," the director admitted. "But it is the only thing we can do. We can't send fellows like Carlos home to certain death. We have to try to save them."

One by one they called in the students whose reports had been positive. When they told Carlos that he had tuberculosis and must be isolated for special care, he did not think of himself. "What about my church?" he asked anxiously. "Will someone take care of my church for me?"

"We'll send another student to pastor it until you are well," the missionaries promised.

"Can I keep on studying?" Carlos asked. "I'd like to finish this year if I could, since we are so close to the end."

"If you feel like it, you can keep on studying," they promised.

Carlos was as disciplined a patient as he was a Christian. He faithfully followed the course of rest and medication the doctor prescribed, and recovered sooner than most of the others. He kept up with his studies and graduated with his class.

His first assignment as a full-time pastor was to a small church in the lowlands—an area completely different from anything he had ever known before. Warm, humid, semitropical in climate, it was like going to a foreign country for the young man from the altiplano.

Carlos did not hesitate to accept his assignment, but he admitted frankly that he was frightened. "I have no idea what it will be like down there," he said. "I'm scared!"

It was probably just as well he didn't know what it would be like, for there were one or two members in the little church who did not like having a young boy fresh from Bible school as their pastor, and they told him so quite frankly.

For his second assignment Carlos was sent to the frontier town of Caranavi to a new preaching point. The church was just one small, dirt-floored room. The pews were planks laid across adobe bricks. But when the missionaries visited Carlos a few months later, the room was filled with people and they were hungry for the gospel message.

During his years as a student pastor, Carlos had met a girl who had gone to the Bible school for one year. She was a devoted Christian, and had remained true to God in the face of much opposition from her people. Now, as Carlos faced his assignment in the frontier town, he thought of Margarita again. He wrote her a letter and asked her to marry him.

Evidently Margarita remembered Carlos favorably too, for she accepted his proposal.

Carlos and Margarita are devoted and faithful servants of God in Bolivia. Wherever He chooses to send them, they will be worthy representatives of Him, for they have learned to trust and obey the leadings of the Holy Spirit.

3

GUYANA

Voice in the Night

David Bansod stepped off the last bus from George-
town and walked away into the blackness of the tropical
Guyana night. His steps were heavy, like the steps of
an old man bowed under the weight of his years. No
one meeting David in the darkness would have dreamed
that he was scarcely nineteen years old.

He lit a cigarette, but the taste was nauseating,
as all of life had become for him. He flung the cigarette
from him.

The sand of the dirt road grated under his feet.
There was no moon, and the streetlights ended at
the bus stop, but David did not need light. He had
followed this road nearly every night as he returned
to his father's house. For what? He wondered cynically.
To sleep awhile, and then set out on another empty
round of drinking and gambling with friends as dissolute
as he was, trying to fill up the hours of one more
purposeless day.

For three years this had been the pattern of his life, and now, suddenly, David was fed up with everything. He had walked out on his friends tonight. Walked out in the middle of a game, without any warning or explanation. What explanation was there to give? How could you explain to friends with whom you had spent nearly every night for three years that you were suddenly sick to death with all of it?

You couldn't. So he had simply pushed back his chair and left.

But now what? Where could he find anything that would take the place of these things with which he was surfeited? What else did life have to offer? Marriage? Yes, he could marry. There were girls around. His parents would be glad to arrange a marriage for him. But for what? To bring children into the world for the same kind of meaningless existence he was living? What would be the use of that?

A career? It was out of the question. Real careers that were worth working for were beyond his reach. Who ever heard of anyone on his social level being a diplomat or a business tycoon? That was only for rich men and their sons. The best he could ever hope for was a job as a clerk in a store, or as a bookkeeper in a factory or a sugar mill somewhere. A great career! Slave all day to provide barely enough food for one's family! Or, if he chose to stay single, to work eight or ten hours a day for a little money to gamble away in an hour or two the same night!

Somewhere in the darkness a clock in a church tower chimed twelve. Funeral bell, he thought mirthlessly. It might as well be. He stopped at his father's gate and leaned against it. Why go in? Why go anywhere?

Behind him in the stillness of the night he heard the sullen roar of the Demerara River sweeping past on its inexorable journey to the sea. He turned impulsively, crossed the road, and stood on the river-bank. It must have rained somewhere in the interior, for the river was running bank-full. A star appeared through the clouds, and the oily blackness of the surging current reflected its twinkling light.

David stared down at the rolling water. One step, and he could disappear forever beneath its powerful flow. Why not? he thought suddenly. One step, and he would be at peace. The struggle to find meaning in life would be over. One step! He felt the mystic pull of the river's surging current drawing him like a magnet.

Then out of the darkness he heard a voice: "David Bansod! Don't throw your life away. If you don't know what to do with it, give it to Me. I can use it."

He stepped back from the river, startled, and peered toward the road. Who could possibly have seen him on a pitch-black night like this?

"Who's there?" he demanded nervously.

There was no answer—no sound of any living creature, save the crickets chirping in the grass near his feet!

At the sound of his own voice, he knew. It was God who had spoken to him. But how did one give his life to God? He had no desire to be a temple priest, ringing bells and saying prayers all day long. Were there other ways of devotion perhaps? He walked slowly back to his home. Tomorrow he would begin his search for the answer to that Voice.

In the morning David surprised his father by accompanying him to the Hindu temple for worship. He prayed the prayers he had learned as a boy. He clapped his hands to waken the gods. He listened closely to the chanting of the priests. But his heart remained empty. He returned the next day, and every day for several weeks, hoping that by the sheer discipline of faithful worship he would find peace. But it did not come.

Perhaps I have been looking in the wrong place, he thought as he passed a Catholic church one day. The Voice that spoke to me that night may not have been one of our Hindu gods. Perhaps it was the Christian God. I never thought the Christian God was for the Indian people, but maybe He is. I'll try that church and see if I can find peace.

So he went to the services in the big cathedral the next Sunday. He watched the priests as they chanted the Latin ritual of the service. He listened to the choir. He bowed his head when the others prayed. But his heart was as empty when he left as it had been when he came. He returned to the church each week for several months, but there was no answer to his quest.

Where does a man find the God whose Voice spoke to me by the river? he wondered, desperately. How can I give Him my life if I can't find Him? Is this just another twist to the mockery that has made life unbearable?

Frustrated in his search, he turned back to his old activities. What was the use of seeking any longer? He hated Christianity. He hated Hinduism. He hated all religions that pretended to offer peace and happiness, but gave only empty husks to the sincere seeker for truth. The Christian God had no more to offer than the gods of the Hindus. Both were powerless to help a man!

As he walked the street in his black mood, he met an old friend whom he had not seen since their school days together. Even then he had seen that there was something different about him. Serenity—that was the word that described him. Meeting him now, when he was older, the contrast between his friend's serene spirit and David's own bleak despair was startling.

"What makes you so different?" David demanded. "You're not like anyone else I have ever known."

40

"I'm a Christian," the friend said cheerfully. "Christ makes all the difference in the world. You need Him, just as I did."

"I don't know what I need," David answered moodily. "I am searching for a Voice that spoke to me one night on the bank of the Demerara River, and stopped me from taking my life."

"Tell me about it," his friend said encouragingly.

David told him of his experience by the river, and of his vain search for the God of the Voice in the days that followed.

"That was the Christian God!" his friend exclaimed confidently. "He will forgive your sins and your wasted life, and give you peace. No other god in the world can do that. Why don't you come with me to my church tonight? You can find God there."

"I'm sorry, but I couldn't," David replied. "I promised my father I would go to the Hindu festival with him tonight. I can't disappoint him."

"Will you come with me next Sunday then?" his friend asked.

"Oh, I don't know," David said slowly. "I've already been to a Christian church. I went several times. It didn't help me. Why should I expect to find God in your church?"

"I did," his friend said quietly. "Come with me, and see if you don't hear that Voice speak to you again."

"Well—" David hesitated. "All right, I'll go with you Sunday."

He had no faith that his friend's God was the One he was seeking, but he was willing to go, if only to prove that his friend was wrong. Could it be possible that the Voice he had heard was not the voice of God at all? he wondered, as he walked toward home. But even as he wondered, he knew he was wrong. It had been the voice of God. Whether it was the Christian God or some other, he did not know, but somewhere

41

there was a God, and when he found Him, he would know.

At the evangelical church the next Sunday the preacher said very plainly that Christ, the Son of God, could forgive any man of his sins and give him peace. Any man!

"Come and kneel here before God and confess your sins," the preacher invited. "Let Him give you peace such as you have never known before."

David considered the man's words thoughtfully. If this were the God he was seeking, he would have to go down and pray, to find Him. But how could he be sure this was the one? The words at the river seemed to echo in his mind: "Give your life to Me."

I might as well try one more time, he thought. Tears of desperation filled his eyes as he walked down the aisle to offer his life to God. How does a person approach this God? he wondered. The prayers he had offered to the Hindu gods did not seem adequate. Finally he began to talk to God as directly as God had spoken to him at the river.

"God of the Christians, are You the one who told me at the river to give my life to You? If You are, and if You are here, I give You my life. I don't know how You can use it, but if You can, You're welcome to it."

Even as he prayed he felt the heavy burden lift from his spirit. He looked up at the Christians kneeling around him. "He has come," he said in wonderment. "This is the God who spoke to me before. I know His voice."

He stood up, and his face shone with joy. "If I could only get my parents and my friends to understand and seek this God!" he said. "My father has sought for peace for years!"

He tried to tell his parents of the miracle that had come to his life, but they were only baffled by his words.

It was beyond their comprehension that a strange God could do more than their centuries-old gods could do. They were not even sure that he was talking about a god. His words did not make sense to them.

The next Sunday David took his younger brothers and sisters with him to the evangelical church. They loved it and were eager to go again.

His father did not object the first time they went. But when they went again the next Sunday, and the next, and then began to talk at home about the Bible stories and songs they were learning, he became alarmed.

"This must stop!" he said agitatedly. "We are Hindus. You must not take these children to the Christian church again. That religion is all right for the English and the Negroes, but it is not for us. The religion of the Indian people is Hindu!"

"The Christian God is for all people," David answered. "He sent His Son to die for all of us. He loves everyone—even you. And He will give you peace, just as He has given it to me."

"Don't link yourself with those Christians!" his father retorted. "You are a Hindu and the son of a Hindu. You can't change the religion into which you were born, any more than a leopard can change its spots."

"Maybe I can't, but God can," David said. "Through the power of God I have been born again into a new life—a new faith."

"You seem to forget that I am the head of this house," his father replied angrily. "I am the one who determines the religion our family will follow. I will not tolerate such false teachings. Either you return to our Hindu faith or I'll put you out of the house and we will mourn you as one who is dead."

David did not reply. There was nothing to be gained now by antagonizing his father further. When his father's anger had cooled, he would try to talk to him again.

43

For several months David walked in joyous communion with Christ. Then one day, when some of his former friends met him on the street, they began to make fun of him for going with the *evangelicos*. David's temper flared. He answered them angrily. The bitter animosity he felt in his heart shocked him. This was not the way a Christian should feel! He prayed for forgiveness, and thought that all was right again. But a few weeks later, when a fellow worker tried to shift the blame for a costly error onto him, the same angry feeling flamed in his heart. He lashed out at the guilty one with bitter words that he regretted as soon as they were spoken. He prayed in anguish for God to forgive him. How could he ever be an effective witness to the grace of God if he could not control this ugly spirit in his heart!

He battled with it constantly. Just when he would think he had it under control, something would happen and it would flare up again. He began to wonder if his father was right, and this Christian religion was not for Indians after all. Yet he knew that God had forgiven his sins the night he knelt at the altar. Surely he thought, if God could forgive after I had done wrong, He must have some kind of grace that will help me not to do wrong in the first place!

He prayed and fasted many days, begging God to take from his heart the ugly spirit that made him act as he did in times of stress. He searched his Bible for help. Through its pages the Holy Spirit led him into the experience of heart purity.

He soon proved that this was indeed the grace he had needed. The day after God cleansed his heart he met his former cronies in the marketplace and they began to scoff and jeer at his Christian faith. If this had happened two days before, David knew he would have struck out angrily in his own defense. But this morning there was no anger in his heart. He only smiled and testified to them of the wonderful miracle of grace that Christ had wrought in his life. The scoffers were silenced by his unexpected response. It made them uncomfortable. They mumbled a few halfhearted answers and scattered.

Shortly after David was sanctified, the Church of the Nazarene began to hold services in his village. He visited their small rented hall, and discovered that they preached the very experience he had so recently discovered for himself. He continued to attend, and finally joined the Nazarene church.

He married Anna, an Indian girl, and settled down in a small rented house near the church. He secured a position in the office of a sugar estate, which provided them with a modest living. For the first time in his life David felt that he had happiness and security and real hope for the future. He could think of nothing more that he desired.

But God desired more for David. As David prayed and read his Bible each day, he became aware that God was calling him to preach the gospel. He was surprised, but he did not rebel. There were many opportunities to preach on Sundays and often during the week as well. He kept his job for financial security, and did his best to preach wherever opportunity offered.

But he had an uneasy feeling that there was something else that God was trying to tell him. He prayed for guidance and the Holy Spirit whispered, "I want your whole life. I want you to go to the Nazarene Training College and prepare for full-time service."

"But, Lord," David argued, "I have a wife to support. We hope to have a family someday. I can't just quit my job and go off to Bible college without any way to support my family."

"I'm here," the Lord reminded him. "You can trust Me."

David did not tell Anna about his battle, but she knew that something was wrong. She questioned him until he finally confessed what the struggle was about.

"But what would we do?" she asked. "How would we live?"

"That's what I keep asking," David said. "I don't see how we can possibly give up our security and go to Bible college. It doesn't make sense. People don't do things like that. What kind of Christian example would I be if I quit my job and let my wife suffer just so I could go to school?"

It was obvious that human reasoning was on David's side. But God was not looking at the problem from the human point of view. He continued to remind David that His will was for him to go to Bible school.

For eight years David and Anna struggled with God's call to enter Bible school. They didn't refuse to go. They just kept presenting all the reasons why they couldn't do it, and stayed where they were.

Then one year at youth camp they went to the altar and settled the issue. Whatever the cost, they promised God they would obey Him. They enrolled in the Bible college at Trinidad and trusted God to help them earn the money they needed. God saw them through, just as He had promised He would.

Four years later they graduated from the college with scholastic diplomas. But more important still, they left with a deep confidence in God's ability to take care of them in any circumstance as long as they were obedient to His will.

They returned to pastor the Grove Church of the Nazarene in Guyana. God blessed them, and soon they had several new preaching places in the communities around the village of Grove. People throughout the area knew the zealous Nazarene pastor. He was liked and respected by people in all walks of life.

Many times over the years David has been reminded of the Voice that spoke to him by the Demerara River that night, saying, "Don't throw your life away. Give it to Me. I can use it." And he has been amazed and humbled as he has seen the way in which God has unfolded His part of that promise.

4

ECUADOR

God Wanted Mr. Nobody

"Here comes little Mr. Nobody," the older boys chanted, laughing and pointing at five-year-old Cesar. "No mama, no papa—just Mr. Nobody!"

"I do, too, have a mama and a papa," Cesar retorted.

"Who are they then? Name them!" the boys taunted.

"Tia Ana and Tio Jorge are my mama and papa," the little boy said, close to tears.

"They're not your mother and father, silly," the older boys said. "They are your aunt and uncle."

"They're my mama and papa," Cesar insisted.

"Then why do you call them Tia and Tio?" the boys demanded. "Your cousins call them Mama and Papa, but you don't. You know why? Because they are your aunt and uncle, that's why. You don't have any mama and papa, Mr. Nobody!"

Cesar burst into tears and ran from his tormentors. He found Tia Ana in the kitchen.

"Tia Ana," he cried breathlessly, "**you are** my mother, aren't you?"

"Just as good as," she answered, rhythmically chopping onions on her board.

"But you're really my mother, aren't you?" Cesar insisted. "Just as you are Susana's and Angel's mother?"

"Almost," Tia Ana said, "but not quite the same. You weren't born mine, but you came to live with me when you were a tiny baby."

"Then who are my real mother and father? Where do they live?" Cesar demanded.

"How should I know?" Tia Ana answered irritably. "Your mother lives somewhere in Ecuador, I suppose. She moves around all the time. I don't keep up with her. And I know nothing about your father. What difference does it make to you? You had parents. Isn't that enough?"

"But who are they? Why don't I live with my mother?"

"Well, if you must know, Mr. Curiosity-Box, your father wouldn't own you, and your mother didn't want you. So I took you to live with me. And when you are old enough to go to school, you'll go to live with Tia Noemi, because I can't afford to buy your school supplies. I have my own children to take care of. Does that satisfy you? Now run along and stop pestering me."

Cesar stared at her in shocked dismay. How could these things be true? He had been sure she was his mother. He stumbled outside and slumped down against the eucalyptus tree in the patio. Big tears rolled down his cheeks. The boys were right. He had no mother and no father. No—it was worse than that. He had had a mother and a father, but they didn't want him. He was worse than a nobody. He was a nobody that no one wanted—not even Tia Ana. She was going to send him away as soon as he was old enough to go

49

to school. He lay down on the hard ground and sobbed until he fell asleep, exhausted.

Cesar did not venture out of Tia Ana's yard again that day.

When he woke the next morning, he was almost sure that the happenings of the day before were just a bad dream. They couldn't be true. He ran outside to play with his friends. Everything was just as it had always been until the older boys came by. Suddenly one of them spied Cesar. "Why, there's little Mr. Nobody!" he said, grinning. "Who's your mother today, Mr. Nobody?"

"Stop calling me that!" Cesar shouted. "I'm not a nobody."

"Mr. Nobody! Mr. Nobody!" the boys chanted gleefully.

When Cesar's playmates saw how it bothered him, they joined the others, dancing and shouting around him.

In an anguish of embarrassment, Cesar pummelled his way through the crowd of tormentors and fled to the safety of Tia Ana's patio.

But Tia Ana had little sympathy with her small charge. "What are you doing sulking around here?" she demanded, when she found Cesar huddled in a corner of the patio. "Go out and play with the other children."

"I don't want to play," Cesar mumbled.

"Are you sick?" Tia Ana demanded, feeling his forehead. "You don't seem to have a fever. Run along outside and play now. I don't want you around here getting in my way." She pulled him to his feet and propelled him firmly through the patio gate.

Cesar went back to his playmates with dragging feet. But they had already forgotten their mischief, and received him into their games without any comment.

Cesar tried to play where the older boys would

not see him, but usually before the day was out some mischievous boy or girl would remember and cry, "There's Mr. Nobody!" And Cesar would cringe in shame and embarrassment because he had no mother like the rest of the children.

It was several months later, when Tia Ana called Cesar in from his play one afternoon. "Come, Cesar, and let me wash you," she said briskly. "Tia Noemi is coming for you this afternoon. I want her to see you clean, once, at least."

She scrubbed him and dried him with a rough towel, then dressed him in a clean pair of trousers and a shirt. On the table in a neat pile were his other clothing.

"Am I leaving here?" Cesar asked, troubled. "Won't I ever come back?"

"It's time for you to start school," Tia Ana said brusquely. "I told you you were going to live with Tia Noemi when you went to school."

"But who will I play with at Tia Noemi's?" Cesar asked. "Tia Noemi doesn't have any children, does she?"

"You won't have much time to play at Tia Noemi's," Tia Ana said. "You will have to work for her to pay for your keep, and you will have studying to do besides. You'd better work hard. Tia Noemi has a very hot temper. If you make her angry, you'll find she has a ready stick to beat you with."

"Do I have to go to Tia Noemi's?" Cesar pleaded. "I'd rather stay with you, Tia Ana."

"And grow up as ignorant as a burro?" Tia Ana scolded. "No, indeed! You have to go to school. And I can't afford to buy your uniforms and your books and such things when I have my own children to take care of. It's all settled. You are going to Tia Noemi's. Now go and sit down somewhere and see if you can stay clean until Tia Noemi comes."

Cesar went outside and sat on the low bench beside the door. He didn't remember Tia Noemi very well.

She had been at Tia Ana's a few times. But she scolded a lot, and he and his cousins had learned to stay out of the way until she went home. Now he had to go and live with her every day. Cesar's small heart was filled with dread.

Tia Noemi came in the middle of the afternoon, soon after siesta time. She visited with Tia Ana while they sipped mate and ate a sweet roll. Then the dreaded moment came. She gathered up Cesar's small bundle of clothing and came outside.

"Come, Cesar," she said sharply. "If you are coming home with me, we might as well get started."

She marched determinedly down the street with Cesar following her.

Even the older boys did not dare to shout, "Mr. Nobody," when Tia Noemi was there. They just watched silently as Cesar trudged past.

Tia Noemi and Cesar boarded a bus at the corner and rode across the city to Tia Noemi's home.

Tia Noemi's home was different from Tia Ana's. There was no front yard at all. The house sat right next to the sidewalk. The front windows were covered by shutters. Tia Noemi unlocked the door and led Cesar inside.

"You will sleep here," she said, showing him a tiny room with a cot in one corner. She put his bundle of clothing in a chest under the window. "Here is your *guardapolvo* [dust catcher]," she said, holding up a new, white cotton school uniform. "I made you two of them. See that you take care of them and don't get them dirty the first day. I have plenty to do without having to wash school uniforms every day. And here is your pencil and paper and a notebook. Use them carefully. These things cost good money. I don't know where I'll get it from, but I promised I'd send you to school, and I'll do it. I don't know why your mother couldn't have kept you and paid for it herself, but she didn't."

"You can send me to my mother if you don't want me," Cesar said timidly.

"No, I can't," Tia Noemi answered shortly. "She doesn't want you either. You'll just have to make the best of it here with me. And see that you work enough to help a little bit with your keep. Now take off those clean clothes, and I'll show you some of the things I'll expect you to do while you live here."

Tia Noemi had more space behind her house than many of the neighbors, and every inch of it was put to good use. There were flower beds in a border around the edge, and a small vegetable garden in the center.

When Cesar came out of his room, Tia Noemi showed him the gardens. "Your job will be to keep the flowers and vegetables free from weeds," she said. "Every day you will spend some time weeding and hoeing. Then there will be errands to run when I need you, and you will sweep the steps and the sidewalk each morning. You might as well start in the garden right now. I'll take you to school tomorrow and find out which session you will be in."

Tia Noemi left Cesar in the garden and went into the house. Cesar looked at the rows of vegetables. He had never worked in a garden before. He wasn't sure which were weeds and which were good plants, and he was afraid to ask Tia Noemi. He dropped on his knees and looked at the green, growing things. Finally, he decided that the larger plants must be the vegetables and the smaller ones weeds. He pulled out a few and sat back to look again. The row looked all right, so he crawled ahead a few inches and pulled some more.

Tia Noemi came out in a little while to inspect his work. "You missed some!" she scolded. "Don't start out being careless. I want every weed pulled. Now come back here and go over this row again."

By this time Cesar had begun to recognize the spinach leaves. He went back to the beginning of the row and pulled out everything that did not look like spinach. Tia Noemi watched him awhile, then returned to the house.

Cesar's shoulders ached, and he was thirsty. He wanted to ask Tia Noemi for a drink of water, but he was afraid to stop working.

At last Tia Noemi came to the door. "You can stop now," she said. "Come in and wash your hands. I want you to go to the grocer's for me."

Cesar scrambled to his feet and went in. "Please, Tia Noemi, may I have a drink?" he asked timidly.

"Of course," she said. "You don't have to ask me for every breath you draw. Get yourself a drink."

Cesar was glad to tumble into bed after supper was over. He did not wake up again until Tia Noemi shook him at daybreak.

"Hurry and get dressed," she said. "I want you to run down to the baker's for breakfast rolls."

At seven-thirty, Tia Noemi helped Cesar put on his *guardapolvo,* and they walked to the school a few blocks away.

Tia Noemi was very pleased when the principal assigned Cesar to the afternoon session. "That will work out very well," she said. "You can work for me in the morning, and go to school in the afternoon. You will have time for your homework after you get home in the afternoon."

Cesar had little time for play at Tia Noemi's. Six days a week he got up at daybreak to weed and hoe in Tia Noemi's garden, and to do her errands. He went to school from one o'clock until five, and then had to come home and do his homework for the next day. Even the first graders had writing to practice and simple sums to do at home. If he finished his schoolwork before suppertime at eight o'clock, Tia Noemi always found something for him to do.

Cesar missed his friends that he had known at

Tia Ana's. There were no children his age in the homes near Tia Noemi's. In fact the building beside Tia Noemi's house was not a home at all. It was a hall—a Protestant chapel, Tia Noemi said.

"You stay away from there!" she admonished sternly. "They are *evangelicos*. We don't associate with *evangelicos*."

Cesar was filled with curiosity. What are *evangelicos*? he wondered. Do they look like other people? As he worked in Tia Noemi's garden, he kept his eyes and ears alert for any sign of the strange people who used the building next door.

For a whole week there didn't seem to be anyone around there when Cesar was in the yard. Then on Sunday morning he saw them coming. There were children and grown-ups. He peeped through the crack in the fence to look at them. He was disappointed. They didn't look any different from Tia Noemi or him. They had light brown skin and dark hair, just like his. They talked Spanish just like he did. And they were laughing and chattering together as though it were fun to go to the funny little chapel.

Cesar hurried to finish his weeding. Tia Noemi had gone to church, and she would be sure to inspect his work when she returned. When he was done, he brushed his hands on his trousers and slipped around the end of the fence to get a better look at the *evangelicos*.

"Hello!" some of the children said, smiling at him. "Have you come to go to Sunday school with us?"

Cesar backed up and shook his head. "I just wanted to see what you looked like," he stammered.

The children laughed, but it was a warm, friendly laugh. "Do we look funny?" they asked. "We're just like you. We even go to the same school you do. Won't you come to Sunday school with us?"

Cesar hesitated. He knew Tia Noemi would be angry if she found out. But she would not be home from church for a while. Perhaps he could go and get back home before she did. He decided to risk it.

They took him with them into the little chapel. He listened in wonder to the singing and the prayers and the stories. He had never heard anything like this before in his life. The teacher welcomed him warmly, and the children smiled at him and made room for him to sit on the bench beside them. They made him feel like someone very special.

The pastor shook Cesar's hand when he went out after Sunday school. "What is your name, Son?" he asked.

"Cesar," he answered, stiffly. Now it will all be over, he thought, dreading the pastor's next question. He'll find out that I haven't any parents, and then no one will want me to come anymore.

"Cesar—?" the pastor waited for Cesar to give his last name.

"Just Cesar," he said miserably. "I live with Tia Noemi—right there on the other side of the fence."

"I see," the pastor said, squeezing Cesar's hand. "Isn't that wonderful? You live close enough to come every Sunday. We hope you will."

Cesar looked up at him in amazement. He was almost sure the pastor had guessed why he didn't want to give his last name. But he didn't seem to care at all. He acted as though he really wanted him to come back. The warm, good feeling of being wanted swept over Cesar from head to toe. He smiled at the pastor. "I'll try to come," he said.

At school the next day Cesar saw some of the children he had met at the *evangelica* Sunday school. "Cesar!" they cried, "come and play with us."

He ran to join them. It was good to have friends again. He began to look forward to going to school each day.

The next Sunday, Cesar got up early without Tia Noemi having to call him. After breakfast he went right to the garden and began to work. He wanted to finish it before it was time for Sunday school.

Tia Noemi looked out in surprise. It was hard to believe that a boy would go to work without being told. Probably wants to play later, she thought. I'll have to find more for him to do. She put on her hat and went to church.

As soon as she was out of sight, Cesar hurried in and washed his hands. Then he slipped around the fence and waited for his friends to come to Sunday school.

Sometimes, when Tia Noemi did not need him to run errands after school, Cesar played with the pastor's children from the *evangelica* church. He liked to go to their home. It was a cheerful, friendly place. The pastor and his wife loved their children, and Cesar felt included in their love when he was there. He found excuses to go to their home whenever he could.

Not all of the boys and girls in the school were friendly. And some who had been friendly at first became unfriendly when they discovered that Cesar was going to the *evangelica* church. They made fun of him. It made Cesar very angry. When they said ugly things about the pastor and his children, Cesar wanted to defend them. He didn't cry and run away as he used to do when he was a little boy. He clenched his fists and struck at his tormentors with all his might. More than one boy went home with a black eye from Cesar's furious attacks.

Sometimes Cesar was the one who had the black eye. When this happened, he knew he would get a beating when he reached home. Tia Noemi did not like fighting. She made sure that the punishment he received when he got home was always worse than anything that happened to him in the fight. Cesar would never

57

tell her why he fought. But he did not stop fighting, for he had to defend his friends.

When Cesar was eight years old, the *evangelicos* had a special meeting just for children. It was in the afternoon after school. Cesar was afraid he would not be able to go, but God intervened in his behalf. Tia Noemi went to sew with a friend that afternoon, and she did not get home until it was dark.

Cesar hurried through his work and slipped around the fence to the little chapel. There was a visitor speaking that day. He talked to the boys and girls about giving their hearts to Jesus. At the close, Cesar and two or three others went to the front to pray. Cesar accepted Christ as his Saviour that afternoon.

He did not understand all that went with being a Christian, but he knew there were some things that would have to be different. He knew he must be honest, and not lie to Tia Noemi, not even to escape a beating. He knew he must not shirk his work, no matter how tired he was. And when Tia Noemi asked him to do errands, he knew he must do them willingly. It was not easy to do these things, but he wanted to live as the pastor said a Christian should.

He went to Sunday school and church as faithfully as he could. If Tia Noemi knew that he was going to the *evangelica* chapel, she did not say anything.

About a year after Cesar accepted Christ, the pastor told the church folk that he planned to have a baptismal service on Sunday afternoon. He explained what the meaning of baptism was to Protestants. "Any person who knows his sins have been forgiven and that Jesus is his Saviour may be baptized," he said. "It is a wonderful way to give public testimony to our faith."

"May I be baptized?" Cesar asked the pastor after the service.

"What about Tia Noemi?" the pastor asked kindly. "Will she let you do this?"

"I don't know," Cesar answered. "But I want to be baptized anyhow. I want to let people know that I am an *evangelica* Christian."

"Don't you think you should talk to Tia Noemi about it first?" the pastor asked. "I think she would be very unhappy if you were baptized without telling her you wanted to do it."

It took a lot of courage for Cesar to talk to Tia Noemi about being baptized. He prayed very hard for God to help him. All week he tried to find a time when Tia Noemi was in a pleasant mood. Finally, on Friday, when he came home from school, he found Tia Noemi in the kitchen preparing a mutton stew for dinner. "I would like to be baptized next Sunday at the *evangelica* church, Tia Noemi," he said quietly.

She stopped stirring the stew and looked at him, startled. "You what?" she said, not believing she had heard him right.

"I want to be baptized," Cesar repeated.

"What kind of nonsense is this?" Tia Noemi demanded. "I know you have been sneaking off and going over there on Sundays, but this is too much. Of course you can't be baptized by the *evangelicos*. You were baptized when you were a baby. When you are twelve, you'll be confirmed in your own church."

"But the *evangelica* church is my church," Cesar said bravely.

"Nonsense! What does an eight-year-old boy know about one church or another? You were baptized into our church, and that is where you will die. Just forget all this ridiculous talk about the *evangelicos*."

She slammed the lid on her kettle and stalked out of the kitchen.

Cesar walked away thoughtfully. He had expected she would answer like this. But what was he to do now? He wanted very much to be baptized. He watched his chance, and when Tia Noemi was busy in the kitchen again, he slipped out of the house and ran to the pastor's.

"I told Tia Noemi," he said soberly, "but she says I cannot have her permission to be baptized. She says I was baptized when I was a baby."

"Do you think you should wait until you are older, Cesar?" the pastor asked quietly.

"No, sir," Cesar answered. "I know we are supposed to obey our parents, but I think this is different. If I told Tia Noemi that I was a Christian, she would forbid me to come here to church ever again. But I would feel I should come just the same. I think being baptized is like this. Even though Tia Noemi won't give her permission, I think God wants me to be baptized. Will you let me?"

The pastor was thoughtful for a moment. "If you were an adult, I wouldn't hesitate for a minute, Cesar," he said after a while. "And in this case I think you are being very grown-up in your thinking about the whole situation. I believe you know what you are doing, and what Christian baptism means. If you want to be baptized next Sunday, I will be glad to have you come with the others."

Cesar did not say anything more to Tia Noemi about it. Nor did she mention it again, either. The next Sunday afternoon she went to visit her sister and left Cesar to look after himself. He went to the service and was baptized with the other Christians.

When Cesar was twelve years old, Tia Noemi decided that he was big enough to begin earning part of his living. She inquired here and there for someone who needed a boy to help him. Finally she found what she wanted.

"Cesar," she announced to him when he came home from school, "I have found you a job. You will go to work for Senor Valdez at his stall in the open-air market tomorrow morning. The hours are very good for you. You will go to work at three o'clock in the morning and work until nine or ten. You won't earn a lot, but it will help some. Whatever you earn, you will bring to me, of course."

"When will I study?" Cesar asked anxiously.

"You will be home by ten-thirty in the morning," Tia Noemi said. "If you study hard, that ought to be time enough. And you can study some after school, if I don't need you for other things."

Cesar worked very hard at the market. He swept out the tiny booth, trimmed the vegetables, and helped Senor Valdez put the heavy baskets of produce on the stands. He waited on customers when Senor Valdez was busy. By the time he was through work at ten o'clock he felt like going to bed rather than hurrying home to study for school.

It was hard to keep up with his classmates when he was tired. Sometimes when he was supposed to be studying, he fell asleep. When he received his first report card, after he had begun working for Senor Valdez, he saw with dismay that he had one very bad grade on it. He was afraid to show the card to Tia Noemi. He kept it as long as he could. But before he went to bed that night, Tia Noemi said, "Isn't today the day you receive your report card, Cesar? Where is it?"

Trembling, he took it out and gave it to her. She glanced at it and turned on him furiously. "You know better than to bring home a grade like this!" she stormed. "I've told you that any grade that is unsatisfactory means a whipping. Why didn't you study?"

"I try to," Cesar said. "I just get so sleepy I can't remember what I read."

"Don't lie to me!" Tia Noemi screamed, reaching for her leather strap. "You just don't want to work. You expect me to feed and clothe you while you play around like a child! You're old enough to work, and you're old enough to study. You might as well learn right now

61

that you can't get away with a trick like this. Every time you bring home an unsatisfactory grade, you will get a beating that you won't forget!"

She lashed him with the leather strap, raising ugly welts on his back and arms and legs. Blood trickled from the places where the heavy strap cut the flesh.

Sobbing from pain, Cesar crept to bed without his supper.

The angry welts were still swollen on his arms and legs the next morning. He looked at them, wondering how he could hide them from the eyes of his friends. He was embarrassed to go to school looking as he did.

"Don't get any ideas about skipping school, young man," said Tia Noemi sharply, as she saw him looking at the ugly red marks. "You are going to school today and you are going to stay there. I shall see to that myself."

When it was time for him to leave, Tia Noemi walked all the way to the schoolroom door with Cesar.

He went inside, filled with embarrassment and shame. All day he sat with his head on his desk and wept. His teacher watched him with concern. When school was over, she walked home with him for fear that he might run away.

Never again did he receive a grade as low as that first one had been. Cesar was not sure whether he was somehow able to remember better, or whether the teacher took pity on him and did not mark him as severely as she had, but at least the grades were better.

By the time Cesar was fourteen, Tia Noemi seemed to take it for granted that he was going to attend the *evangelica* chapel. She even gave him permission to go to their youth camp for a week's vacation. It was at the youth camp that Cesar yielded his life to God and was sanctified. The Holy Spirit began to talk to him about preaching the gospel. But Cesar did not want to preach. He wanted to be a Christian, but there were other things he wanted to do in life instead of preaching. He worked at various jobs that year, but none of them satisfied him.

Finally, he decided that he would go to Bible school —not to prepare to preach, but to secure an education so that he would be qualified to look for a better job than he was able to get now.

He got a job in one of the Quito shoe factories to help him with his school expenses. He worked hard and well, and soon was promoted to be a supervisor. He was proud of his new position. It was not as high as he hoped to go someday, but it was a promising beginning.

But one day the manager of the factory discovered that shoes were disappearing from Cesar's department. Cesar was blamed. Without being given any chance to defend himself, he was immediately fired.

It was the last straw on the stack of personal problems that had been piling up in Cesar's life as he tried to run from God's will. He could not stand any more. He ran away to Guayaquil on the coast, where no one knew him. Here, he thought, he could begin life over again. He went to work in a distillery, but he was miserable. He shifted from job to job, but he was restless and unhappy in them all. Nothing that he tried seemed to satisfy him.

Finally, heartbroken and bitterly discouraged, Cesar went back to Quito. He had no home there, or anywhere else, but he went to the home of one of his Christian friends, and they took him in. He found a job and worked for a little while, then shifted to another, and then to still another. None of them satisfied him.

Wherever he went—whatever he did—God was always there, quietly, gently, but persistently reminding Cesar that God's plan for his life was to preach the gospel.

After months of running away, Cesar finally reached the end. He felt he could run no longer. The time had come to face up to the issue that was haunting him. Either he must give up his faith in God and turn his back on the Christian life or he must accept God's call and preach the gospel. He spent the night in prayer, battling it out. By morning he had made his decision. He went back to Bible school, to prepare to preach the gospel.

5

PERU

Like a Two-edged Sword

"Tomas is drunk again!" The flock of barefooted children chanted the words like a nursery rhyme as they scrambled up the path to Maria's little adobe hut. She was sitting on the doorstep.

"Pedro says to come down to the *tambo* and take him out of the way." Squealing and laughing, they scampered off to resume their games.

Maria sighed heavily. She walked with heavy steps down the path that meandered through the little mountain village. At her brother-in-law's house, she stopped.

"Miguel," she called.

Luisa came to the door.

"Is Miguel here?" Maria asked.

"In the daytime?" Luisa said acidly. "Not likely. He's at the *tambo* drinking chicha with all the other good-for-nothing men of this village. If every man here went away and never came back, there'd be just as

65

much work done as there is now, and we'd have twice as much to eat besides!" She went back inside the house and slammed the door.

Maria went on down the path to the little shop where Pedro sold chicha and aguardiente. Through the open space at the top of the slatted swinging doors, she could make out the dim forms of the village men lounging about inside. The clink of bottles and the bursts of loud laughter told her that they had been drinking for some time.

She stepped up to the doors. "Miguel," she called loudly.

A man detached himself from the group and came outside.

"I've come for Tomas," Maria said. "Bring him out and help me get him home."

Miguel stepped back inside and in a few moments reappeared with the limp form of Maria's husband. They draped the drunken man's arms over their shoulders and half-carried, half-dragged him up the dusty path to the windowless sod hut that was Maria's home. There they rolled him onto his pallet in the corner and left him. Tomorrow he would waken, sullen, morose— and penniless.

Maria felt in the sleeping man's pockets. "I suppose he tore up his money as usual," she said bitterly. Sometimes she was able to salvage a little money for food while Tomas slept. But more often his pockets were empty. The first few swallows of aguardiente made Tomas feel like a millionaire. With grandiose gestures he would pull out the few soles he had left, tear them into bits, and scatter the pieces in the air.

She shook her head hopelessly.

Miguel said nothing. He went back down the path to rejoin the others at the *tambo*. He was sorry that his brother drank as he did. But there was nothing he could do about it; or about his half-starved kids either, for that matter. It was just the way things were; that was all.

Everyone in the village of Chaupilanche was poor; but Tomas, with his drunken millionaire dreams, was the poorest of them all. Indeed, if his brother Miguel had not slipped a sack of beans or corn inside the door once in a while, the family would have starved for sure.

It didn't occur to Maria that there could be a better way to live. Most of the village women shared the same lot to some degree. They didn't expect anything better. If the good Lord willed them to be poor, what could anyone do about it?

They planted their small gardens, and if the rains came right, they harvested their peas and corn and turnips and potatoes. Sometimes they had a scrawny pig or goat. If they had any extra vegetables or livestock, they took them to the market in Chota, a few miles down the mountain. With money realized from the sales they bought salt, sugar, and sometimes a bit of new cloth for a dress or a shirt, or a pair of tire-tread sandals for the rocky trails.

Coming home from his trip to the market one day, Miguel found himself on the loneliest part of the trail, as a mountain rainstorm swept down upon him. He was soaked in minutes. The path became a slippery quagmire. In the swiftly falling darkness, it was foolhardy to go on. One false step would send him over the precipice to certain death on the rocks below. He looked about him desperately for shelter. No one lived anywhere near, he knew. Then, half-hidden under a thorn tree, he spied an abandoned adobe shanty. He struggled through the soggy underbrush and crept inside. The building was dark and old, and there was no wood with which to build a fire for warmth. But it was dry, and there was some protection from the icy mountain wind that moaned outside. He huddled under his wet poncho and waited miserably for the morning.

As the first light of the new day crept in through the broken door, Miguel looked up at the wooden rafters that supported the roof of his shelter. Gradually his eyes made out an odd shape on one of the cross timbers. What could that be? he wondered. It looked like a small, flat package wrapped in brown paper. Could it be money, or some other valuable loot hidden there long ago by a mountain bandit, and forgotten?

He straightened out his stiff, cramped legs and shinnied up the post. Seizing the package, he slid to the floor and eagerly pulled open the wrappings. It was only a book. Disappointed, he peered at the black cover. Across the top were faint gilded letters. He spelled them out slowly. "*S-A-N-T-A B-I-B-L-I-A.*"

"A Bible!" he muttered. He dropped the Book as though it had scorched his fingers. He had never seen a Bible before, but the priest had warned him about it. This was the Book of the terrible *evangelicos*. It was a sin to read it, and a worse sin to try to understand what it meant.

Miguel trembled as he sat in the presence of this evil thing. But he was curious, too. What strange words might be in this mysterious Book? He remembered, suddenly, hearing a man on the street in Chota one day say that the Bible contained the secret of a better life.

My brother Tomas could profit by this secret, Miguel thought soberly—if there is indeed a secret here. And I wouldn't mind having a better life myself, though I don't need it like Tomas does.

He looked at the black Book before him for a long time. He longed to see the mysterious words on its pages, but he could not muster the courage to open the covers. After a long time he wrapped the Book again, climbed up the post, and put it back into its hiding place. Whoever had hidden it there probably would come back and get it.

Suddenly a thought struck him. What if it belonged to Satan himself? Miguel slid down the post and scurried from the hut. He glanced back over his shoulder fearfully to see if the devil might even now be lurking in the dim shadows. Pulling his still-wet poncho about him, he hurried as quickly as he could up the muddy trail toward home.

But he could not get the black Book out of his thoughts. Who could have put such a Book up on the rafter in the old abandoned hut? Had the devil done it to tempt him? Or could the Book really be good, as the man in Chota had said? Had God let it be put there for him to find and learn the secret of a better life?

He said nothing about his discovery when he reached home, but he thought about it often. His curiosity grew until he could scarcely stand it. He made up his mind that when he went to Chota again he would stop and see if the Book was still there. If it was, he would bring it home and see, once and for all, what was inside its covers.

Almost as though the priest knew what was going on in Miguel's mind, he announced the very next Sunday that a special fiesta would be held in honor of the village patron saint. In all the excitement of planning and enjoying the dancing and the costumes and the drinking at the fiesta, the Book was forgotten.

It was several weeks before Miguel went to Chota again. But one day, when he needed a new shovel, he had Luisa gather a few vegetables and he set out for the city market. He sauntered along the trail, planning what he would buy with the money he received from his sales. Suddenly he came to the empty hut.

"The Book!" he exclaimed half-aloud. "But I can't take it now. Someone would surely see it and ask questions. I'll stop and get it when I come back." He passed on down the trail without stopping.

The market was crowded with many sellers and it took Miguel awhile to find his counsin Dona Carmen among the throng of women displaying their wares.

"I have a few things here," he said, after greeting her. "Will you sell them for me?"

Dona Carmen agreed readily. Nothing was said about her pay, but both of them knew that a part of all she received from his sales would find its way to her own private funds.

Free from responsibility, Miguel joined the men visiting near the *tambo*.

Selling was slow, but it was good. Dona Carmen was able to bargain for an excellent price on everything Miguel had left with her. But it was late in the afternoon when she turned the money over to Miguel. He hurried about the market buying sugar, and a handful of nails, and his new shovel.

The shadows of the buildings were already half across the narrow street when he had finished. He cast an anxious eye toward the sun as he packed his purchase into his *alforja*. He would have to walk very fast to reach home before dark. To stop at the abandoned hut on the mountain now would be unthinkable. No man in his right mind would linger on the bandit-infested trail with darkness coming on.

Clouds began to form around the mountain peaks above him. Miguel saw them and tried to quicken his steps. Darkness was bad enough, but to be caught on the trail in a chill mountain rainstorm was worse.

But he was too late. Just as he reached the empty hut beside the trail, the storm broke. There was no question then about stopping. He ducked inside out of the downpour. It was already so dark that he could not see the rafters above his head. He huddled down in the corner in his soggy poncho and prepared to spend the night.

In the morning he looked up. The package was still in its hiding place! He climbed the post, retrieved the Book, and tucked it inside his *alforja*. He trembled with excitement and apprehension as he stumbled on up the trail in the foggy half-light of the early dawn.

If this Book was a trap of the devil, what would happen, he wondered. Would Satan send a landslide to push him off the trail to his death on the rocks far below? Would bandits attack him—or a tree fall and crush him to death? He walked warily, watching for danger on every side.

Slowly the mists cleared away, the sun broke through the ever-present clouds, and Miguel's fears subsided. Suppose this Book were indeed the Word of God, as the man on the street in Chota had said. It could very well be a protection from evil!

As soon as Miguel reached home, he hid the package where no one would find it. It would not do for anyone in the village to know that he had a Bible. The priest would certainly be angry with him and probably would demand that he bring the Book to be burned. He didn't want this to happen until he had at least had a chance to look at it.

When darkness fell and the villagers were all inside their own homes, Miguel lit his homemade lamp and sat down to read the Book. The smoke from the chimneyless cooking fire hung low in the room, making his eyes smart. Slowly he spelled out the words, syllable by syllable. He stopped frequently to think about their meaning. The little guinea pigs that were grown for the family's meat supply, and were pets as well, scrambled unheeded over his bare feet.

As Miguel read, he became excited and troubled at the same time. These things are not wicked, he said to himself. They are good. But if they are good, then the priest is wrong, and the man in the market at Chota was right.

This was something to think about a long time. If it were true, it could upset their whole lives. He continued to read and ponder.

After several weeks he talked to Tomas about the Book. "You ought to read it," Miguel urged. "It would make you a better man."

Tomas took the Bible home and read from it himself. "It is good, indeed," he said to Miguel. They began meeting together, sometimes in Miguel's home, and sometimes in Tomas'. Their wives worked about the house as the men read from the Book. They said nothing, but they listened to the words and to the discussion of the men.

"This Book says many good things," Tomas said at last. "But it also has many things in it that I don't understand. I wish there were someone who could explain it to us."

"The *evangelicos* could explain it," Miguel said slowly, a little aghast at his own boldness. "They have a chapel in Chota near the market, you know."

"But if we were seen going there we would be in great trouble with the priest," Tomas answered. "And who would dare to venture inside their place? You know the terrible things that go on there."

Miguel nodded. "But the priest was wrong about this Book," he said slowly. "Do you suppose he could be wrong about the *evangelicos* too?"

"I'd be afraid to try to find out," Tomas said. "Everybody says they are bad."

Luisa was not quite so sure about the danger. She had heard enough from the Book to be convinced that it spoke the truth. And she knew enough about village gossip to realize that the stories about the *evangelicos* could well be false. She said nothing to the men, but she began to scheme for a way to get to Chota and find out for herself.

"I need some more salt, and some needles," she announced the next week. "I have some potatoes and corn that I can sell. I think I'll go to the market today."

Miguel went with her, for like most mountain men, he did not like to let his wife go away from home alone. Luisa sold her vegetables, and then walked from stall to stall bargaining for the things she wanted. "I'd like to go by the livestock market on the way home," she said. "I've been thinking about buying a small pig, if I can find one."

She followed her husband to the animal market beside the *evangelica* church. As they drew near, they heard the Protestants singing.

"Listen," Luisa said, as though she had only then discovered the church was there. "They're singing. I wonder what is going on."

They stood still a moment on the street outside the gate.

"They are singing about God and the Cristo," Luisa said after a moment. "Such beautiful words!"

"Come on," Miguel said fearfully, looking about him. "We must not be seen standing here." He started on down the street.

"But the Bible is good. You said so," Luisa remonstrated, following him. "If they believe the Bible and teach it, isn't it reasonable to think that they are good too?"

"I don't know," Miguel said agitatedly. "I don't know what to think. But until we do know, we must be very careful."

Luisa was silent. There was no point in arguing. But she determined that she would find a way to come back someday and find out what these people really had to say.

A few weeks later she heard the village women talking about a *norteamericano* missionary who was

73

coming to the chapel of the *evangelicos* in Chota. She pretended utter disbelief.

"Ha! A missionary come all the way up into the mountains to Chota?" she scoffed. "I don't believe it. Why would they leave the cities on the coast for this difficult place?"

"Well, it's true," the talebearer insisted, nettled by her neighbor's disdain. "My husband brought a piece of paper home from the market yesterday that told about it. I read it myself." She was very proud of her ability to read.

"Oh, you did!" Luisa said scornfully. "And just when is this great person coming, then?"

"Three weeks from last market day," her informer said triumphantly. "I can bring you the paper and show you—if you can read it."

"I can read it," Luisa said hotly. "But you needn't bother to bring it. I'm not about to have a paper of that sort in my house. And if you don't want to get into trouble with the priest, you'd better get rid of it too."

She turned and walked away, as though she wanted to hear no more on such a dangerous subject. But inside she was gleeful at her success. She had learned all she wanted to know, without revealing her interest at all. She began planning how she could get to Chota while the missionary was there.

She counted the days carefully. On the right market day, she said to Miguel, "I'd like to go to market today. It has been more than a year since Mother died. I'd like to get out of this black garb and wear something colorful again."

"*Ay, mujer!*" Miguel teased. "You are always wanting to spend money. Do you have any?"

"Yes, a little," Luisa answered, smiling. She was glad he was in a pleasant mood.

74

"Very well, if you'll buy something for me too, I'll take you with me."

She laughed. "Good. I'll buy you something to eat— something you really like."

"It's a bargain," Miguel said. "Put on your shawl and come along. But don't tease me to buy everything you see."

They both dressed in their best for the trip to Chota. Miguel wore his white duck trousers, loose in the leg and tight at the cuff. Over them he put his worn brick-colored poncho. He put on his new sandals made from old auto tires, and his wide-brimmed sombrero. Luisa wore the black mourning skirt she had worn for more than a year, and wrapped her black woolen shawl about her arms and shoulders to protect her from the wind and sun. She too wore a wide-brimmed sombrero.

They walked down the mountain trail with Miguel in the lead.

When their vegetables were sold, they strolled around the market searching for a piece of bright cloth for Luisa's new dress. They enjoyed seeing the wares of the merchants, and were in no hurry to buy. At last Luisa found what she wanted. She tucked her purchase inside her shawl and they walked on.

"Let's go by the animal market again," Luisa said. "Maybe today there will be a small pig that is fit to buy."

As they came near the white adobe church of the *evangelicos*, Luisa exclaimed, "Look at the crowd! I wonder what is going on."

They paused, looking curiously at the open door, through which they plainly heard the voice of someone preaching.

"That's a stranger," Miguel said. "He doesn't speak like one of us."

The pastor, standing at the church door to keep the children from running in and out, saw the thin little man with his plump wife, listening at the gate.

75

He walked out to speak to them. "Won't you come in?" he invited.

Luisa looked eagerly at her husband. This was what she wanted to do very much.

But Miguel stepped back frightened. He was terrified to have an *evangelico* so close to him.

The pastor knew the fear that filled his heart. He did not urge Miguel to come. He visited with them casually, talking about the weather, the market, and the prospects for a good harvest. Miguel answered him guardedly.

At a pause in the conversation, the voice of the preacher came to them clearly.

"He speaks very good Spanish for a *norteamericano*, doesn't he?" the pastor said casually.

"A *norteamericano*?" Miguel said curiously. "How did he get way up here in the mountains?"

"He lives down in Chiclayo, but we invited him to come and speak to us. He is very interesting. Wouldn't you like to step inside and hear him better? It is quite crowded but I think there is a little room to stand just inside the door."

Luisa almost held her breath. Miguel was torn between fear and curiosity. He wanted to hear this strange *norteamericano* who spoke Spanish so fluently— but would he dare step inside the *evangelicos'* church? Surely in a crowd this large they would not dare to try any of their terrible deeds.

Hesitantly he stepped forward. Luisa pressed close behind him so that he could not step back if he wanted to. Trembling, Miguel climbed the four giant steps that led to the barren little church. He slid inside the door and looked quickly around for the stations of the cross, the high altar, the confession booth with which he was familiar. There were none of these. The room held only a few benches and a pulpit on a high platform where the missionary was talking. He was holding a black Book like the one Miguel had been reading.

The benches were filled with attentive people—men sitting on the left and women on the right.

"Ssss!" Luisa whispered, tugging at Miguel's poncho. "Take off your sombrero."

He looked around. All the men had taken off their big hats and piled them in the window recesses along the thick adobe walls. He pulled his off and held it in front of him. Suddenly he recognized the wife of the leading doctor in Chota sitting near the front. Near her was Dona Mercedes, one of the best-educated women of the city. Among the men he saw prosperous merchants sitting side by side with poor people like himself. Even the town *palomilla* (smart aleck) was there, listening as intently as the rest. What would bring people like this together, he wondered.

Once in a while someone stood up to rest a moment before sitting down again on the hard wooden seat. Sometimes a listener would bend over to scratch a troublesome flea bite, but no one took his eyes from the speaker. Even the children seated on the floor in front turned their round, solemn little faces upward in rapt silence as they listened to the missionary.

At the close the missionary invited people to come to the front and ask God for salvation from their sins.

Miguel was convinced that this man spoke the truth. He knew now that what he had read in the Bible was true. There was salvation from sin; he needed it, and he could have it by praying to God directly. But he was afraid. He trembled, but now it was from conviction for his sins.

Pastor Garcia spoke to him gently. "Give your life to God," he urged. "He can forgive your sins and give you a new life. You can have peace in your heart."

Miguel wanted desperately to accept the invitation but he could not bring himself to walk down the aisle to the front. Luisa waited anxiously. She wanted to pray, too, but she could not unless Miguel did.

Pastor Garcia guessed why Miguel was hesitating. "Would you kneel right here where you are and ask God to forgive your sins?" he asked.

"Yes," Miguel answered, and he and Luisa knelt down by the door.

The pastor prayed with them and they opened their hearts to the Lord. There were no tears. It was almost like a business transaction. They believed what the missionary had said and what they had read in the Bible. They followed the pastor's instructions, and when they had done as he told them they believed that God forgave them, just as He had promised He would.

Quietly they rose from their knees and thanked the pastor for his kindness. They walked out into the street and started home.

But though there had been no visible transformation, there had been a wonderful change wrought in their hearts. All the way home they talked about their new peace and joy.

"Tomas must hear of this," Miguel said. "This is just what he needs. Only God can deliver him from his drinking. We must get him to the evangelical chapel, where he can hear about the saving power of Christ."

Tomas listened intently that night as Miguel explained what Christ had done for him and Luisa. Everything that Miguel said fitted in with what Tomas had read in the Bible. He was ready to believe. He repented and received Christ as his personal Saviour too.

It did not take the villagers long to know that something had happened to Miguel and Tomas. They no longer took part in the drinking bouts and the fiestas. They didn't beat their wives and children. They were honest in their business transactions. The little money that Tomas earned was used for food for his brood of half-starved children. Miracles like this could not escape the attention of anyone.

But the villagers were not glad for the change in these men. They were angry and afraid. They did everything they could to try to make them turn back to their old ways. Vile stories were told about them, accusing them of many things. Their children were cursed and spit on as they walked in the streets. Their chickens were stolen. When one of Tomas' children died some weeks later, the entire village insisted that it was a punishment from God.

But in spite of the abuse and the sneers and accusations, there was one thing no one could deny: Miguel and Tomas were different and better men.

Gradually, as their goodness impressed the villagers more deeply, the antagonism melted away. Men became ashamed to attack these two who did nothing but good.

Word filtered through the village that Miguel and Tomas studied the Bible at night in their homes. One after another, the villagers found excuses to drop in on them. They stayed to listen to the reading of the Book.

In a few years a little adobe chapel was built, with a shining, corrugated-iron, "Alabaster" roof. A number of the villagers found Christ and began serving Him. The children of Tomas and Miguel gave their hearts to Christ also. One of Tomas' sons was called to preach the gospel and went to the Nazarene Bible College.

Thus one small, black Book—the Word of God—cut through the village of Chaupilanche like a two-edged sword—and the lives of the village people will never be the same again.